MIGRATION

*First published in the United States
in 1992 by*
Gloucester Press
95 Madison Ave
New York, NY 10016

Library of Congress
Cataloging-in-Publication
Data

Parker, Steve.
Migration / by Steve and Jane
Parker.
p.   cm. — (Animal
behavior)
Includes index.
Summary: Examines
different kinds of migratory
movement and the animals
that use them, from birds and
butterflies to the great
whales.
ISBN 0-531-17311-9
1. Animal migration—
Juvenile literature.
[1. Animals—Migration.]
I. Parker, Jane 1951-   .
II. Title. III. Series: Animal
behavior (New York, N.Y.)
QL754.P32   1992
591.52'5—dc20
92-9831   CIP   AC

Printed in Belgium

Steve Parker is a writer and
editor in the life sciences,
health and medicine, who has
written more than 50 books for
children on science and nature.

Jane Parker has a degree in
zoology and has worked as a
researcher at London Zoo. She
now works as a publishing
researcher and indexer.

Design: David West
Children's Book Design
Designer: John Kelly
Editor: Jen Green
Picture researcher: Emma Krikler
Illustrator: Adrian Lascom

Photocredits
All the pictures in this book
have been supplied by Bruce
Coleman Limited apart from
the following: pages 7, 11 top
and 21 top: Planet Earth
Pictures; page 14: Natural
History Picture Agency.

ANIMAL BEHAVIOR

MIGRATION

STEVE & JANE PARKER

GLOUCESTER PRESS
New York · London · Toronto · Sydney

CONTENTS

INTRODUCTION 5

LEARNING OR INSTINCT? 6

PREPARING TO MIGRATE 8

READY, STEADY... 10

FINDING THE WAY 12

TOO COLD OR HOT? 14

FOLLOWING FOOD 16

BREEDING MIGRATIONS 18

NORTH-SOUTH MIGRATIONS 20

MIGRATING UP AND DOWN 22

DAILY MIGRATIONS 24

IRRUPTIONS 26

ANIMAL NOMADS 28

SPOT IT YOURSELF 30

GLOSSARY 31

INDEX 32

INTRODUCTION

Migrations are special journeys. They involve large numbers of animals traveling over great distances. These journeys usually follow a regular pattern. Migrations are quite different from the small-scale, random wanderings of a creature's daily life.

Most areas of our planet experience seasonal changes. Warm summers give way to cold winters, and dry seasons are broken by rains. Some animals can cope with these fluctuating conditions. They do not leave the environment in which they live. They are residents.

Other animals cope with changing conditions by traveling to places where the situation is more favorable. These journeys involve the mass movements of many animals, over relatively long distances. The journeys often follow a regular pattern, and the animals behave in a special way while traveling. These creatures are migrants. Many types of animals migrate, from tiny insects to great whales. Birds are great migrants. About 4,000 kinds migrate every year — half of all bird species.

Why migrate?

In temperate regions such as Europe and North America, spring and summer are warm and sunny. Most animals feed well and rear their young at this time. But winter is cold, and there is little food. Some creatures avoid these harsh conditions by migrating to warmer places. They return the following spring.

In polar regions, reindeer, harp seals, and whales also travel in autumn to warmer, temperate areas.

Other creatures migrate to avoid predators. Manatees are large aquatic mammals. In the flooded Amazon River region, they graze on vegetation. But as the floods subside, they risk being stranded in pools, and caught by predators such as jaguars. They migrate to deeper lakes, where they are safer.

The Arctic tern holds the record for long-distance migration, flying halfway around the world twice yearly.

LEARNING OR INSTINCT?

Many mysteries surround the process of migration. How do animals know when and where to migrate? In some species, the young follow older, experienced adults. But other animals on their first migration manage to find the way correctly on their own.

Swans are long-lived birds, and the accumulated experience of the flock helps to guide new fledglings on migration. Their V-shaped flying group is called a skein.

Japanese cranes breed in marshes and lakes in summer, and fly south to avoid severe snows.

Flying high
Red-crowned cranes from northern Japan raise one or two young each year. The parents guide their offspring on their first southerly migration to winter feeding grounds. The crane flock flies in a V formation or in single file, the youngsters following the older birds. The young birds learn the route, and also save energy by flying in the slipstream of the bird in front.

Learning and memory play an important part in migration in most large animals, such as mammals and big birds. During the brief summer in Siberia, swan parents raise a family of cygnets. As autumn approaches, the swan families begin their migration, flying thousands of miles to spend winter in warmer regions farther south.

Swans live for many years, and the experienced parents guide their offspring on the long flight. The young learn the route and landmarks, and they can usually make the journey themselves within a year or two.

Built-in behavior
Other migrants, such as small birds, and butterflies and other insects, must have a built-in or instinctive "knowledge" of their migration. They make the journey without a guide, reach the correct destination, and return again. How?

Scientists think that the information is somehow contained in these animals' genes. Genes are present in all the cells (the microscopic building blocks) of the body. Genes are passed from parents to young and from one generation to the next. They provide all the instructions for building an animal's body, from its overall shape to its skin color. The genes also contain information on how the creature should behave – including how to migrate.

On best behavior
Many animals change their normal behavior for migration. Spiny lobsters of the west Atlantic usually live alone, hiding in a favorite crevice. Each lobster fights other lobsters that come near, and competes with them both for food and for territory.

But at the first autumn storm, these creatures behave in a very different way. They line up in their thousands, to move to cooler, deeper waters. They travel nonstop for several days, covering up to 10 miles each day. Each lobster keeps in touch with the ones in front and behind by feel and sight. They even cooperate, defending each other from predators by gathering in a circle, with their tails together and their claws facing outward. In deep water, safe from waves, they slow down to use less energy while food is scarce.

Pastures new
In some species, migration is not a regular event. Animals simply set off when they are forced to, by over-crowding, food shortage, drought, or some other difficulty.

Wildebeest (gnu) live alongside zebra and antelope on the African grasslands. They eat only grass, and in the dry season, when this has all withered or been eaten, they must find new pastures. The wildebeest join together into huge migrating herds, tens of thousands strong. Somehow they can sense where rain has fallen and new grass is growing. The herds swim wide rivers and climb steep hills. Hundreds of animals perish during the journey.

The urge to move on in search of water is so strong that wildebeest will tackle the most rugged terrain.

PREPARING TO MIGRATE

Migrants must be well-fed and in peak condition before their journey begins. They use huge amounts of energy on migration, yet they may not be able to feed while traveling or even at their destination. Some species must be ready to breed as soon as they arrive.

Blue whales spend summer in polar seas, and winter in the tropics. These mammals tend to breed in the open sea.

Most animals eat extra food before migration. They digest it and store the "spare" energy as body fat, under the skin and between the body parts. This is like a jetliner taking on extra fuel before a very long flight.

The great whales are the biggest eaters. They use the whalebone plates inside their mouths to sieve small shrimplike creatures, krill, from the water. Krill feed and breed near the sea's surface during the short Arctic and Antarctic summer. A big whale can consume more than two tons of krill every day! During this time it puts on enormous amounts of fatty blubber, up to 20 inches thick, under its skin.

The polar summer is brief, however. The days shorten, the oceans turn cold, and the krill die off. The whales migrate toward the tropics for the winter. Here the seas are warmer, but contain no krill. The whales survive on their layers of fatty blubber, eating hardly any food for months on end.

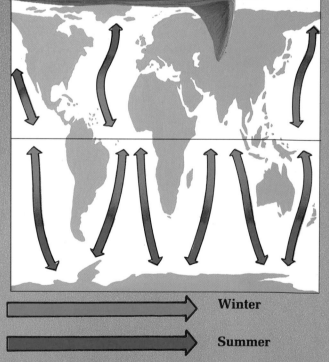

Winter

Summer

Gaining weight
Many wagtail and pipit species breed in Europe, and avoid the cold winter there by migrating to Africa. They travel over the Sahara Desert, flying for several days without food or rest. The meadow pipit is only 6 inches long. Before it sets off, it eats enough insects, worms, and seeds to double its body weight!

Some pied wagtails remain in Britain all year. Others fatten on insects and migrate.

Golden plovers breed in the northern summer, and fly thousands of miles south in great flocks for the winter. Some leave North America and head for Argentina. Others cross the Pacific from Siberia to Australia. American golden plovers are among the migration record-holders, with flights as long as 8,000 miles.

Before their great journeys, golden plovers change their feeding behavior. They visit marshes and open country, and fatten up on insects and shellfish. During migration they lose up to one-quarter of their body weight.

Camouflaged among the grass stems, a golden plover feeds in preparation for its journey.

The strong survive

Nature's law is "the survival of the fittest." Migration is the chief hazard that some creatures face, and only the strong and healthy live through its hardships. The sick and old, and many of the young, die on the journey. This seems wasteful, but it helps to ensure that the animals making up a species stay fit and strong, and are well suited to their life-style.

Long-distance fliers depend on their wings, particularly during migration. Birds preen themselves to make sure that their plumage is in good condition. Many species molt their old feathers and grow new ones before they start.

Baby dogfish spend up to ten months inside their protective case before they hatch.

Nursery waters

Sometimes young animals are prepared for migration, even when the parent has gone. Dogfish are small sharks that live in coastal waters. Each year, females mate and then migrate to the shallow water near the shore, to lay their eggs. Eggs and young in deeper water would be at risk from other dogfish and sharks who cruise there.

A dogfish egg has a tough case with curly tendrils on each corner. When washed up empty on the shore, it is called a "mermaid's purse." The tendrils catch onto rocks or seaweed and hold the egg steady, while the baby dogfish grows inside, nourished by plentiful yolk. When it hatches, the young dogfish is alone, but being well-nourished, it is soon ready to head out to sea.

READY, STEADY...

The timing of an animal's migration usually depends on the cues it receives from its surroundings. For a seasonal migration, reliable cues include changes in daylight hours and temperature. Other animals begin their journeys when food becomes scarce.

Animals searching for new sources of food or water set off on their migration when they get hungry or thirsty. Since rainfall is often seasonal, their movements also turn out to be seasonal. Springbok on the African savannah follow this pattern of migration. Before their herds were decimated by hunters with guns in the 19th century, springbok treks were one of the greatest wildlife migrations on Earth, with herds of 10 million animals on the move.

Other animals time their migrations by detecting clues from their surroundings, which warn of harsh conditions approaching. As the seasons change, the most dependable clues are temperature differences, and daylength – the length of daylight in each day. Swallows gathering on telephone wires in Europe, ready to fly to Africa, are reacting mainly to the rapidly-shortening daylight hours of early autumn.

Swallows take off on short "practice migrations" before they begin their long flight in earnest.

Body clocks

Animals seem to have a biological "clock" in their bodies, which somehow measures time. Scientists believe that they are able to compare the length of daylight time with their own 24-hour clock. When the daylight hours get too short or too long, it is time to leave.

It is possible that the eyes of some creatures, or other parts of the body such as the pineal gland near the brain, respond to daylight by producing a body chemical, a type of hormone. As daylength shortens in autumn, less hormone is made, and this triggers migratory behavior.

Clues from the surroundings

A feature of an animal's surroundings that triggers migration, such as temperature or daylength, is known as an environmental cue. Environmental cues also set in motion other types of behavior, such as hibernation.

Tides, which are linked to the phases of the moon, are used as a cue by some sea creatures. Palolo worms live in tunnels in Pacific island reefs. To breed, the rear end of each worm splits away and wriggles to the surface! There it bursts open to release eggs or sperm into the sea. For increased success, all the worms release their reproductive segments at the same time – on the two days when the moon is in its last quarter, during October and November. The worms may prepare for this mass "migration" by comparing their internal clocks with the changing tides.

Reproductive segments of Palolo worms approach the surface near Fiji, during the breeding period.

Left behind

The blackbird prepares for winter like a migrating bird. It eats well and builds up its fat reserves. But it is a resident – it stays behind, and survives partly by changing its behavior. In summer it eats plenty of insects, but these die off in autumn. During winter the blackbird flicks over dead leaves and searches under them for berries and seeds. It keeps its feathers fluffed up to stay warm. And it roosts for longer periods, in sheltered places such as trees or bushes, to preserve body heat and save as much energy as possible.

The massed herds of springbok on migration were once the biggest gatherings of large land mammals on Earth. Today numbers have fallen, but the treks are still impressive.

The blackbird survives in a snowy landscape, living off windfall fruit and seeds until spring.

FINDING THE WAY

Migrating animals find their way with amazing precision, even if they have never made the journey before and are on their own. Scientists have general ideas about how animals navigate, but many of the details are still unknown.

Animal migrations are astonishingly accurate. Some birds travel thousands of miles and then return to last year's nest site. After years at sea, certain fish find their way to the same small stream where they were born.

These feats are astounding to us. Part of the explanation is that the behavior of many creatures depends on things humans cannot detect, but the migrants can. For example, some animals are sensitive to magnetism, to very low- or high-pitched sounds, to electrical signals, or to types of light that are invisible to our eyes, such as ultraviolet or infrared rays. Some can detect incredibly faint smells or tastes, or even slight changes in gravity. These "super senses" may help them to find their way.

A noisy world

The world is full of sounds we cannot hear. Some large animals, such as whales and elephants, communicate using very deep rumbling noises, known as infrasound. Certain birds, such as pigeons, can hear infrasound, which travels farther than ordinary sounds. Low-pitched infrasound noises are also made by natural phenomena, such as waterfalls, waves crashing on a beach, and wind blowing over hills or through forests. Animals may detect these infrasound patterns and compare them to a built-in or learned "sound map" as they migrate.

Animal compasses and lenses

Many kinds of creatures appear to detect the earth's natural magnetic field with some sort of "body compass." Experiments have shown that a pigeon may lose its way if a small magnet is strapped to its body. The magnet seems to disturb its own magnetic sense. Likewise, migrating whales may go off course and become stranded on the shore in areas where magnetic fields are unusually strong or variable.

A homing pigeon or migrating swallow compares remembered positions of the sun, moon and stars with its internal clock, to navigate at any time of the day or night. It also recalls visual landmarks such as mountains and rivers.

Whales use a variety of navigational methods, possibly including magnetism.

Homing pigeons may find their way using a combination of senses: infrasound and ultrasound, magnetism, ordinary and polarized vision, and the sun, moon and "star maps" in the sky. Millions of years of evolution have made the pigeon's brain and senses well suited to navigation, because its survival literally depends on them.

Many species of insects and birds see light differently to us. Some have built-in "polaroid lenses." Even when the sky is cloudy, they know where the sun is, from the pattern of polarized light.

Smelling the way home

Many animals have a more powerful sense of smell than humans do. Salmon migrate from fresh water to the sea when young. They return to fresh water as adults, to breed.

Each salmon tries to find the exact place where it hatched from its egg. As the adults swim upstream, covering more than 60 miles each day, they may use clues such as salt levels in the water, and magnetism. But the salmon's main guide at this time is probably smell. Each stream has its own combination of chemicals in the water, and the salmon can detect this "smell print" as it returns.

A sockeye salmon leaps a waterfall to reach its spawning stream.

TOO COLD OR HOT?

Unsuitable temperatures are one of the main reasons for migration. In cold conditions food is scarce, and animals may be in danger of freezing to death. Too much heat can be equally hazardous.

Many animals cannot keep going when the temperature becomes too high or low. During a hot summer, creatures run the risk of overheating or drying out in the sun. Harsh winter conditions are just as perilous. In winter, some species of warm-blooded animals enter a special kind of long, deep sleep called hibernation. Many cold-blooded creatures have an inactive, or dormant, stage in their life cycle, such as the egg or pupa (chrysalis) of a butterfly.

Migrants solve these problems by moving out. They travel elsewhere, to avoid great cold or heat.

Head for the hills

In the southeast Australian lowlands, bogong moths lay their eggs in spring. This is a common animal strategy. The increasing warmth and sunshine of spring mean an abundance of plant food for the bogong caterpillars which hatch from the eggs.

The bogong caterpillars grow, pupate and emerge as adult moths. But the Australian summer is too hot and dry for the bogong moths. So these insects migrate high into the Australian Alps. There, temperatures are lower because of the greater altitude. The moths hibernate in dark crevices until the autumn, when it is cool enough for them to return to the lowlands.

In some years, bogong numbers increase. Migrants land in their thousands at resting places.

Swift parents feed their hungry nestlings on insects. Their breeding done, these birds migrate to tropical Africa.

False start

Like swallows, swifts fly to Africa for the winter. These birds can feed, mate and even sleep on the wing. They spend the summer in Europe, where they breed. Their main food supply while raising young is flying insects – cold-blooded creatures that are greatly affected by the temperature.

In a cool spring, flying insects do not hatch out of their over-wintering eggs or pupae so quickly. To begin with, they are scarce. Many birds who arrive back from Africa, and breed straight away, lose their young when this happens. But young swifts can withstand several days of low temperatures with no food. They go into a kind of hibernation until the weather warms, the flying insects hatch out, and their parents are able to feed them again.

Dugongs browse on sea grass. They are the only true sea-dwelling vegetarian mammals.

Winter grazing

Dugongs are sea mammals related to manatees (see page 5). Along western Australian coasts, dugongs spend the summer in shallow coastal waters, eating the lush underwater plants that grow there. However, these creatures cannot stand the cold. As winter sets in and the water cools, they migrate more than 90 miles north, to warmer waters. Here the plants are tougher and less nourishing, but the dugongs do not have to endure the cold.

Reindeer move south to keep ahead of the snows, as winter grips the northern tundra.

In the far North, other mammals also migrate to escape cold conditions. In summer, reindeer graze on the treeless Arctic tundra. For winter, many migrate south to avoid the extreme cold. The reindeer travel in large herds with their young. After hundreds of miles they reach the sheltered northern pine forests and better grazing.

FOLLOWING FOOD

Many animals migrate in search of food. Food supplies vary in abundance with the seasons, but by traveling from one place to another, migrants are able to eat all the year around.

Predators and prey

The type of food an animal eats has a great impact on its life-style and behavior. Plant-eating animals may have to follow the life-giving rains to find fresh grazing. Or they may be forced to leave high mountain pastures as these freeze with winter snow and ice. The meat-eaters that prey on the plant-eaters often follow them. So predators and prey may well migrate at the same time.

Summer flush

In polar and temperate seas, extra nutrients and the long daylight hours of summer mean a "summer flush" of food. This is mainly in the form of tiny floating plants called phytoplankton. Small animals eat the plants, and bigger animals eat the smaller ones, and so on, forming the food chains of the seas.

The summer flush of food attracts many larger marine creatures away from tropical waters near the equator, to spend summer in the northern and southern oceans. The great whalebone whales are one example (see pages 8-9). Another is the requiem group of sharks, whose dorsal fins show above the water as they swim.

Shark migrants

Many requiem sharks migrate long distances. They spend the winter in warm tropical seas, then they swim north or south, to follow their prey into temperate waters for the summer. The requiem group includes famous killers such as the tiger and hammerhead, and the white-tipped sharks.

Hammerhead sharks migrate in pursuit of their prey. In summer they sometimes present a hazard for human bathers in temperate waters.

Bottlenose dolphins range widely from the tropics to temperate regions, chiefly in coastal waters.

Pack ice hunter

Bottlenose whales, like dolphins and other toothed whales, are marine hunters. Many spend winter in the warm waters of the Atlantic off West Africa. In the summer they migrate to the rich waters around the edges of the polar pack ice, in pursuit of the abundant fish which gather to prey on the creatures consuming the phytoplankton there.

Some predatory fish and sea mammals follow their food toward the warm shallows offshore in summer and back out to the deep sea as coastal waters cool in winter. Dolphins track their food of squid and fish on such migrations.

British willow warblers fly more than 2,500 miles in autumn, even as far as southern Africa.

Home and away

Willow warblers nest in Europe, including Britain and Ireland, and in Asia as far north as Siberia. But they feed only on insects, and must travel up to 7,500 miles to reach northern Africa for a sure supply of food during the winter months.

Some warblers that breed in Europe, like the Dartford warblers of Britain, are residents and do not migrate. In a mild winter the species does well, and large numbers of these warblers survive without having struggled to fly long distances, like their migrating cousins. In hard winters, however, the species suffers great losses, because there are so few insects to eat.

Secretive and rare in southern England, Dartford warblers have lost much of their heath habitat.

Most kinds of parrots are permanent residents of tropical forests, where food is plentiful all year. However, blue-winged parrots are an exception. These parrots pass the winter in southeast Australia, where they survive on seasonal fruits and berries. Then they fly 120 miles across the Bass Sea, to take advantage of the summer flush of fruit in Tasmania, where they breed.

BREEDING MIGRATIONS

The migrations of many animals are linked to finding good conditions in which to raise their offspring. The young, and the parents caring for them, need an abundance of food and favorable temperatures. Safety and shelter are also important.

Some creatures have specialized needs when they reproduce. They not only need plentiful food, but also highly oxygenated water, or special nest-building materials, or a suitable place to leave their eggs. The urge to find all these conditions at the same time, in the same place, drives some breeding animals to migrate great distances.

Digging up the beach

The green turtle lives most of its life at sea, usually alone, grazing on sea grasses and seaweed. But the places where the best sea grass grows are not ideal sites for the female turtle to lay her eggs. So every two or three years, after mating, the females swim long distances to the best egg-laying beaches. Green turtles have been migrating to traditional sites in Southeast Asia and the Caribbean for hundreds if not thousands of years.

When they arrive, the females climb laboriously onto the sand, dig deep holes and bury their eggs. The warm sand causes the eggs to develop. When the tiny turtles hatch, they dig themselves out of the sand and scurry down to the sea.

Some of these beaches have become popular with human tourists, and are busy with hotels and roads. The turtles' instincts are so strong that they still come back. Sadly, the loss of safe breeding beaches is a major hazard facing these already rare marine reptiles.

Nursery fjords

Narwhals live around the Arctic pack ice, feeding on squid, crabs, and fish. To breed, these small whales migrate south to fjords – the deep bays and inlets off the coasts of Greenland and Scandinavia. There the young are born.

There is little food in most of the fjords. But the water there is relatively warm, and the narwhals are safe from powerful predators such as killer whales. The adults live on stored body fat, and the young, feeding on their mothers' milk, grow quickly.

The male narwhal has a long spiral tusk, which is a greatly elongated tooth. Calves are dark blue at birth, and only gradually develop the blotched coat and white underbelly characteristic of adult narwhals.

A female green turtle covers up the eggs she has laid on a beach in East Java, Indonesia.

Ospreys (fish-eagles) are found in many parts of the world. Every year they migrate to the same nest sites to raise their young. In some regions, these birds have become very rare, due to human interference.

Japanese salmon

The Japanese ayu is a close relative of the salmon. It breeds in river mouths, and then the young move out to sea, feeding over the winter. The next spring they travel back into the rivers, needing the high oxygen levels of cool, fast-flowing water to complete their development. The ayu's first few years include at least two major migrations.

Every year, many frogs are squashed as they cross roads to get to breeding ponds (above).

Relying on nature

Each spring, frogs and toads return to the pond where they were hatched as tadpoles, to breed. Many other migrants return to their birthplace in the same way. In the natural world, this strategy makes good sense. It is usually better to return to a reliable breeding site, than to try and find a new one by chance. The frog's pond, for example, is still likely to be there, year after year.

But human activities disrupt natural migrations. Frogs and toads try to cross new roads and go around buildings that have been built on their migration routes. They arrive to find that ponds have been filled in or polluted. The frogs' strong homing instincts contribute to their problems in today's world.

NORTH-SOUTH MIGRATIONS

Most animals on migration travel in a northerly or a southerly direction. This is due to the way seasons affect different parts of the world. Migrations to the west or the east are much less common.

The earth is round and spins on its axis once a day. It tilts on its axis as it travels around the sun. These factors mean that daylength, temperatures, and seasons vary in different latitudes north or south on the globe. The differences as you travel east or west are much less marked.

In the tropics, on either side of the equator around the middle of the world, daylength stays much the same all year. The main changes are in rainfall. As you travel north or south, the seasons become more marked. Near the North Pole there is a short summer and a long winter. The South Pole has the same seasons, but at opposite times.

Summer all year around
Some migrants move from temperate lands nearer to the tropics, to avoid the difficult winter months. Others need long hours of daylight in order to find enough food. They can have continuous long days by migrating from the northern summer to the southern summer, as the seasons swap over. The most impressive migrants, long-distance fliers, travel halfway around the globe.

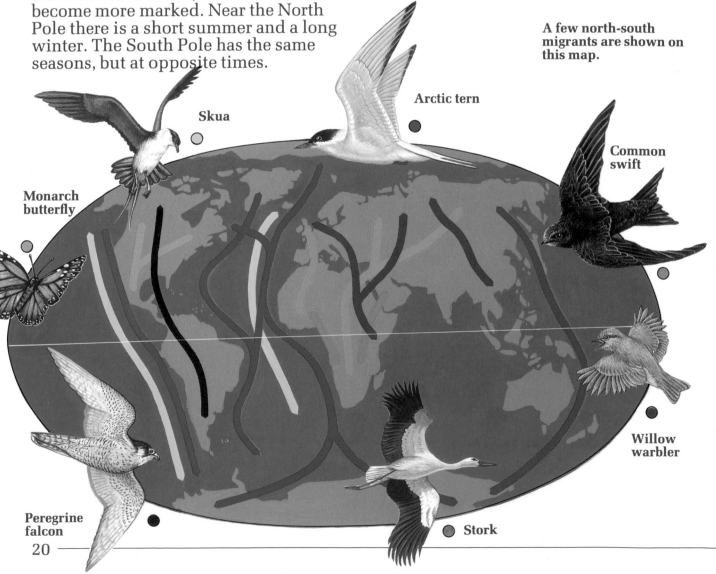

A few north-south migrants are shown on this map.

Skua

Arctic tern

Common swift

Monarch butterfly

Willow warbler

Peregrine falcon

Stork

20

Arctic terns spend long hours in the air on their great migrations. They feed on the route.

Record breakers

Arctic terns are the champion long-distance migrants. They breed in the far north, within the Arctic Circle, during the northern summer when the sun never sets. Then, to avoid the long northern winter when the sun never rises, the terns fly halfway around the world to the Antarctic, to take advantage of the southern summer.

This incredible journey of 9,000 miles is reversed six months later, to coincide with the next northern breeding season. The terns feed on fish that they catch by diving into the surface waters of the sea. Their long flights use up a great deal of energy, but because they migrate, Arctic terns are able to feed throughout the whole year.

Butterfly champions

The monarchs hold the butterfly migration record. They breed in summer in Canada, then fly more than 1,800 miles south, as far as Mexico. These butterflies travel by day, feed on the route, rest at night, and cover more than 62 miles daily.

Swimming along the coast

Gray whales are well-known north-south migrants. They have been thoroughly studied by scientists because they stay near the coast, where they can be tracked and observed.

These huge mammals cover several thousand miles, between their Arctic summer feeding grounds in the Bering Strait, and their winter breeding grounds off California, where the calves are born in the warm lagoons. The northern waters offer more food in summer, while the babies need the warmer waters farther south for their first few months of life.

Biologists follow gray whale migrations by tagging and fitting radio transmitters to these mammals.

Summer breeding, winter feeding

Many raptors (birds of prey) follow the animals they prey on, and migrate north and south, between summer breeding grounds and winter feeding grounds. The long-distance champions are Eastern red-footed falcons, which fly from eastern Siberia to southern Africa.

MIGRATING UP AND DOWN

Like the far north or south, the mountain heights have a short but busy summer, and a long, icy winter. Many creatures spend summer on the upper slopes when food is plentiful, and migrate for winter to the sheltered lowlands far below.

Going up a mountain is like traveling north or south toward the Poles. The temperature drops, winds increase, and rainfall patterns are different from the lowlands. Yet the valleys and lowlands between the mountains are sheltered and mild. Animals that live on the sides of great mountains often move with the seasons. They travel down to escape the worst of the winter, then go back up in spring to take advantage of the summer flush of food.

Benefits and drawbacks

Chamois are agile and sure-footed. They can survive harsh weather and long periods without food. During summer these goat-antelopes graze on herbs and flowers high on European peaks. Few other creatures can reach these heights, so the chamois have little competition for their food. At such great altitudes they are at risk from few predators. But as the temperatures drop in autumn and the snowline creeps back down the mountain, even the chamois must travel lower to find food and shelter.

For the chamois, the benefits of a migratory lifestyle, such as finding plenty of food in summer and shelter in winter, outweigh the dangers and the energy used during the journey. This balancing act is true of any migration. Otherwise the migrations would be unsuccessful, and the migrants would soon die out – or stop migrating.

Chamois are quite at home on the rocky crags and steep rocks of their high-altitude summer feeding grounds.

Deep-frozen grasshoppers

Mountain grasshoppers are usually wingless, unlike many of their lowland cousins. The mountain growing season is so short, and food so limited, that the larvae grow into adults without the "expense" of growing wings.

However, in mild years, mountain grasshoppers breed well, and their usual habitats low on the mountainside become overcrowded. When this happens, some develop wings and fly higher up the mountain, looking for new food. The American migratory grasshopper often does this.

However, in the mountains, weather conditions can quickly worsen. The grasshoppers may be forced to land high up. Sometimes they become too cold to take off again, and then they perish in severe conditions. On Grasshopper Glacier, in Montana, in the United States, thousands of grasshoppers are frozen into the ice. Some of their bodies are hundreds of years old.

The mountain grasshopper (this is a winged form) shows colorful stripes in its defense posture.

Summer heights

Himalayan treecreepers are mountain migrants from the world's highest range of peaks. In summer these birds fly to forests 11,500 feet up on the steep slopes, searching for insects living in the leaves and bark. These insects cannot survive the winter, so they produce cold-resistant eggs or hide as pupae in the autumn. Deprived of food, the treecreepers return to the milder foothills and valleys.

Some treecreepers are residents, others migrate. Most feed on insects and other small animals.

On the opposite side of the world, a small hummingbird migrates for a different reason. Most hummingbirds dwell in tropical forests, but Anna's hummingbird lives in dry parts of California. It breeds in the rainy "winter" season, from November to March. As the summer drought approaches, this tiny bird flies high into the mountains. In the moister conditions there, it can still find enough nectar-providing flowers to survive.

A parent Anna's hummingbird feeds its two chicks in their rainy-season nest.

DAILY MIGRATIONS

The oceans are full of migrating creatures. Seals and great whales travel on their vast yearly treks. There are also many kinds of animals that make vertical trips in the water, moving between the depths and the surface every day.

Plankton floats in the surface waters of the ocean. It is made up of tiny plants known as algae (see page 16), along with microscopic animals, and the minute, developing young of bigger creatures such as fish and shellfish.

These masses of tiny life are the "pastures of the oceans." The microscopic marine algae trap the sun's energy and use it to live and grow, just as grasses and trees do on land. The small plankton animals eat these miniature sea plants. In turn, they are eaten by bigger and bigger fish and by other animals.

A magnified view of plankton, tiny animals and plants that float near the surface of the sea.

The ups and downs of ocean life
Plankton drifts along with the currents, but it also has a daily vertical migration. The tiny plant organisms sink tens or even hundreds of feet by day, then rise at night almost to the surface. Exactly why this happens is not clear, but many little animals follow their rise and fall. Some of these plankton-dwellers are luminescent – they glow in the dark. At night their presence sometimes makes the surface of the ocean shine eerily.

Up from the depths
The deep-sea dragonfish of the North Atlantic also have a daily vertical migration. These strange-looking fish have a light organ on their heads which they use to lure prey toward them. They spend the day at a depth of around 6,500 feet, hidden in the darkness. As evening approaches they swim to the surface, by then also in darkness, to feed on plankton during the night.

Lanternfish live in the mid-depths of the sea, at about 1,600 feet. Like dragonfish, they have light organs, hence their name. These fish migrate upward at night – but only by about 165 to 300 feet. This small distance is enough to put them out of range of possible predators from below, especially the fierce lancetfish that hunt by night in the mid-water depths.

Reef rhythms

Coral reefs support two different worlds: the daylight animals and the nighttime ones. Changeovers occur at dawn and dusk, when the diurnal (daylight-active) creatures swap with the nocturnal "night shift" ones.

Diadema sea urchins lurk in dark crevices deep on the reef face by day. At dusk they leave their hiding places and head upward, moving on their tilting spines and long, thin tube "legs." They climb up to the higher rock shelves and slopes, where they graze on seaweeds during the night. In this way the urchins evade daytime predators that might eat them. They also avoid competition from other seaweed-grazers, who eat the same food by day.

A sea urchin from the West Pacific grazes the mussel-encrusted rocks under cover of darkness.

Night feeders

The builders of the reef, the tiny anemone-like coral animals called polyps, withdraw inside their hard, stony shells during the day. There are too many fish around that hunt by sight, who would soon see the polyps' waving tentacles and nibble them away.

The coral polyps open at night to strain bits of food from the water with their tentacles. Even so, they do not escape all predators. Certain sea slugs, called nudibranchs, lurk at the base of the reef by day. At night, like the urchins, they migrate up the reef to the coral polyps and nip pieces from their delicate tentacles.

Lanternfish have rows of light-producing organs, called photophores, along the sides of their bodies. The glow from these organs may confuse predators.

The nudibranch's bright colors warn potential predators that it is poisonous.

IRRUPTIONS

Animal populations are affected by variations in climate. In some years, conditions are better than usual. Animals breed well and their numbers rise, or irrupt. But as conditions return to normal, they may be forced to embark on a one-way migration.

In most years, lemming numbers are relatively low, and they do not undertake their famous "marches."

Most places on Earth experience a seasonal cycle of weather. Sometimes for a period of years the weather is favorable, and other conditions are also good. Food becomes abundant. Breeding is successful and animal populations go up. Such a population explosion is called an irruption.

This may seem to be a success story – for a time. But eventually it can lead to overcrowding. Food and living space run out, leaving huge numbers of hungry animals. This situation often triggers a spontaneous migration. A large group of animals set off together to get away from the overcrowded area, but with little sense of direction.

The march of the lemmings
The irruptions of the lemmings of northern Europe and Asia are famous.

On the mass migrations that result, the behavior of lemmings can seem suicidal. Yet it is the opposite instinct – survival – that motivates it.

A mother lemming can give birth to several litters (sets of babies) each year. Each litter may contain up to ten young. In good years, therefore, numbers of lemmings tend to rise rapidly. After two or three good years, the alpine pastures can no longer support these greatly increased populations.

At such times, the behavior of these small rodents changes. They move down the mountains in large numbers. If their path is blocked, "lemming jams" build up. In panic, the animals search for any way out, even over a cliff into the river or ocean. Many die, but some find new places to live. Numbers gradually return to normal levels.

Pine wood migrations

Siberian jays live deep in the pine forests of the far north. They feed on berries and pinecone seed. When the climate is consistently mild for a period of years, the birds consume as much food as they can, lay extra eggs, and raise more young.

Gradually the years of plenty cease. The jays' food supplies return to normal, so the extra birds must find new places to live. This happens quite suddenly, and the precise trigger that makes the birds leave is not understood. Hunger, and having too many close neighbors, probably play a part.

Waxwings live in large flocks in temperate coniferous forests. They feed on fruit, flowers, and insects. About every ten years, their numbers build up, and then food runs out. The flocks grow bigger and fly farther in search of food. Many birds die on these migrations. In the traditional folk tales of the regions, the appearance of waxwings, far from their usual territory, is a bad omen.

Massed butterflies

Great southern white butterflies breed all year around on islands off Florida. Their caterpillars feed on vidrillos, a type of woody plant that is common on salt marshes. Every three or four months, the young butterflies which have just emerged from their chrysalis cases fly off to find a new food source. Their departure allows the plants in the old area to recover.

Usually these movements are on a small scale. But sometimes, for no apparent reason, these butterflies take off in dense clouds which look like snowstorms. They may fly more than 62 miles along the coast, to set up new breeding colonies. The "cabbage white" butterfly migrates around Europe and Asia in the same way.

Waxwings' population expansions may be linked to the abundance of one of their foods, rowan berries. In 1965-66, more than 11,000 of these winter visitors "invaded" Britain.

These "cabbage whites" have increased in numbers and are swarming in Kashmir Province, India.

ANIMAL NOMADS

Some species of animals have evolved as wanderers. They migrate and find food wherever and whenever they can, and they are able to breed quickly if conditions are suitable. Vast areas of cropland are sometimes devastated by these animal pests.

Some animals are true nomads, or wanderers. They have no home base. They migrate in large numbers, and settle in an area only as long as food, water, and other supplies last. Then they are on the move again.

Many of these nomadic creatures do not have a breeding season. They can get ready to reproduce very quickly at any time of year, whenever conditions happen to be right. These unpredictable animals tend to live in deserts and other harsh habitats. They are often pests of farm crops.

The dreaded locust plagues occur every few years, whenever conditions are favorable.

Wild budgerigars always seem to be on the move, searching for food and water in twittering flocks.

Outback budgies

Budgerigars and zebra finches live wild in large flocks in the Australian bush. They feed on seeds, and they fly around and settle wherever recent rains have produced a supply of food. If the plants and seeds are plentiful enough, they nest in tree-holes and raise young. When the food has gone, they move on. The adaptable nature of these birds allows them to be kept successfully in cages.

A plague of locusts

Desert locusts have devastated lands in Africa and Asia for thousands of years. These much-feared insects sometimes live alone, almost unnoticed, feeding on grasses. But after long-awaited rain, they start to breed in large numbers. The young thrive on the fresh plant growth, and their behavior becomes quite different. They abandon their solitary lives and crowd together in swarms up to 50 billion strong.

The migrating swarms soon strip huge areas of plants. They darken the skies as they search for more food. They may travel for 3,000 miles, breeding on the way. Cropfields in their path are eaten bare within minutes.

Extra locusts feed the hungry chicks of the wattled starling, allowing it to breed more successfully.

Cashing in on the explosion

Locusts are a favorite food of the wattled starling. This bird lives in the same areas as locusts, and its breeding cycle is closely linked to the locusts' population explosions. When the insects begin to swarm, the starlings quickly come into breeding condition. By the time the baby starlings hatch, locusts are plentiful enough to feed even the hungriest nestlings.

Weather forecasting

Australian emus feed on almost anything – on seeds, fruits, flowers and leaves, as well as insects, worms, and lizards.

Now and then, drought grips the land. The outback dries out in the hot Australian sun. The emus watch the sky for distant clouds and listen for faraway thunder. These birds cannot fly, but gather in large flocks. Then they begin to run, heading toward an area where rain may fall, and where there may be new vegetation and insects. These great emu flocks devour any plants on the way, and can be terrible pests. Farmers erect huge fences to keep them away from crops.

The emus' wanderings may seem very different from the regular journeys of Arctic terns, great whales, harp seals, or monarch butterflies. But all these animals have adapted to changes in their surroundings by migrating. We can marvel at their behavior by watching their movements. But the precise happenings in the bodies of these migrants, which trigger their journeys and enable them to navigate so accurately, are some of nature's best-kept secrets.

Emus become so numerous in certain areas that their numbers are kept down by controlled shooting.

SPOT IT YOURSELF

You can study animals and the way they behave almost anywhere. Learn to detect creatures by the signs they leave: burrow entrances, nests, footprints in mud or snow, hair caught in wire or branches, droppings, half-eaten leaves and discarded shells. Approach animals downwind, so your scent does not give you away. When nature-spotting, keep as still and quiet as possible.

Practical tips for nature-spotting
Wear wind- and water-proof clothing in dull colors. Polaroid glasses reduce surface reflection for seeing underwater. A lens magnifies small animals and a camping mat gives some comfort.

Camberwell beauties arrive for autumn from the north.

Swallows fly south for winter.

A lapwing prepares for winter in the meadows.

Plovers fly south from riverbanks for winter.

A salmon swims upriver to spawn.

Crossbills increase their numbers in woodlands.

Name of animal:
Appearance:
Numbers seen:
Time of day / weather:
Behavior, actions and sounds:

Take a notebook and pencil with you to record your finds outside. A pocket field guide will help you to identify animals.

Take care of nature
When studying animals in natural surroundings, make notes and take photos, but don't capture or frighten creatures. They will behave unnaturally in captivity, or if you disturb them. Take all your litter home with you, and follow the local wildlife laws.

GLOSSARY

Behavior The actions and movements of an animal, including sleeping, feeding, and courting.

Daylength The number of hours of light in a 24-hour day/night period.

Environmental cue A factor in an animal's surroundings, such as temperature or daylength, that triggers changes in an animal's body, or in its behavior.

Evolution Change in species of living things over a period of time, usually over many generations.

Hibernate To become dormant or torpid during the winter months.

Hormone A chemical that travels around an animal's body in the blood, and acts as a messenger between parts of the body.

Infrasound Sounds which are too low-pitched to be detected by human ears, but which many animals (whales, elephants, and birds) can hear.

Instinct A kind of behavior that is "inbuilt" from birth, that an animal carries out without having to learn from its parent.

Irruption A rapid change in population numbers.

Migrant An animal that migrates.

Migration A seasonal or other periodic movement, of relatively large numbers of animals over relatively long distances.

Nomad An animal (or person) with no long-term fixed home base; a wanderer.

Phytoplankton The microscopic plants that drift in the surface waters of oceans and large lakes.

Polar Close to the North or South Poles of the earth, where the winters are long and cold, and the summers are short.

Polarized light Light waves in which the undulating wave motions all occur in the same plane (all up-and-down, or all side-to-side, or all in some other plane).

Predator An animal that lives by hunting others.

Prey An animal hunted for food by a predator.

Pupa The "resting" stage in insects such as beetles, bees, and moths, between the larva stage and the adult insect.

Resident An animal (or person) that stays in the same place for a long period of time.

Species A group of living things with the same characteristics, that can breed together.

Territory An area of land that one animal, or a group, claims and defends against others, usually of its own kind.

Ultrasound Sounds which are too high-pitched to be detected by human ears, but which many animals (bats, dogs, and birds) are able to hear.

INDEX

algae 24
animal pests 28, 29
Arctic terns 5, 20, 21

behavior patterns 7, 31
biological clocks 11
birds 5, 6, 9, 12, 13
birds of prey 21
blackbirds 11
blubber 8
bogong moths 14
breeding sites 18-19, 21
budgerigars 28
butterflies 6, 14, 20, 21, 27, 30

chamois 22
coral reefs 25
cranes 6
crossbills 30

daily migrations 24-5
Dartford warblers 17
daylength 10, 11, 20, 31
diurnal animals 25
dogfish 9
dolphins 17
dragonfish 24
dugongs 15

elephants 12
emus 29
environmental cues 10-11, 31
evolution 13, 31

falcons 20, 21
food as fuel 8, 9
food chains 16, 24
food supplies 16-17
frogs 19

genes 7
grasshoppers 23
green turtles 18

harp seals 5

hibernation 14, 31
homing pigeons 12, 13
hormones 11, 31
hummingbirds 23

infrasound 12, 13, 31
insects 6, 13
instinct 6-7, 31
irruptions 26-7, 31

krill 8

lancetfish 24
lanternfish 24, 25
lapwings 30
learning and memory 6
lemmings 26
locusts 28, 29
long-distance migration 20, 21

magnetism 12, 13
manatees 5
meadow pipits 8
mountain migrants 22-3

narwhals 18
navigation 12-13
nocturnal animals 25
nomadic animals 28-9, 31
north-south migrations 20-1

ospreys 19

Palolo worms 11
parrots 17
phytoplankton 16, 17, 31
plankton 24
plovers 9, 30
polar regions 5, 8, 20, 31
polarized light 13, 31
polyps 25
population explosions 26-7
predators 5, 16, 24, 25, 31
preparations 8-9

prey 16, 17, 24, 31
pupae 14, 15, 31

reindeer 5, 15
residents 11, 17, 31

salmon 13, 19, 30
sea slugs 25
sea urchins 25
seasonal changes 5, 10, 20, 26
senses 12-13
sharks 16
Siberian jays 27
skuas 20
sound patterns 12
spiny lobsters 7
spontaneous migrations 26, 27
springbok 10, 11
storks 20
survival rates 9
swallows 10, 12, 30
swans 6
swifts 14, 15, 20

temperature extremes 14, 15
tides 11
toads 19
treecreepers 23

ultrasound 13, 31

wagtails 8, 9
wattled starlings 29
waxwings 27
whales 5, 8, 12, 16, 17, 18, 21
    blue 8
    bottlenose 17
    gray 21
    navigation skills 12
wildebeest 7
willow warblers 17, 20

zebra finches 28